MONSTERS!

MEDUSA

BY FRANCES NAGLE

Gareth Stevens
PUBLISHING

Please visit our website, www.garethstevens.com. For a free color catalog of all our high-quality books, call toll free 1-800-542-2595 or fax 1-877-542-2596.

Cataloging-in-Publication Data

Names: Nagle, Frances.
Title: Medusa / Frances Nagle.
Description: New York : Gareth Stevens Publishing, 2016. | Series: Monsters! | Includes index.
Identifiers: ISBN 9781482448672 (pbk.) | ISBN 9781482448696 (library bound) | ISBN 9781482448689 (6 pack)
Subjects: LCSH: Medusa (Greek mythology)--Juvenile literature.
Classification: LCC BL820.M38 N335 2016 | DDC 398.2'0938'01--dc23

First Edition

Published in 2017 by
Gareth Stevens Publishing
111 East 14th Street, Suite 349
New York, NY 10003

Copyright © 2017 Gareth Stevens Publishing

Designer: Samantha DeMartin
Editor: Kristen Nelson

Photo credits: Cover, p. 1 Mondadori Portfolio/Mondadori Portfolio/Getty Images; p. 5 Slava Gerj/Shutterstock.com; p. 7 Eye Ubiquitous/Universal Images Group/Getty Images; p. 9 Dimitrios/Shutterstock.com; p. 11 Linda Bucklin/Shutterstock.com; p. 13 Mondadori Portfolio/Hulton Fine Art Collection/Getty Images; p. 15 PHAS/Universal Images Group/Getty Images; pp. 17, 28 Universal History Archive/Universal Images Group; p. 19 Peter Paul Rubens/Wikimedia Commons; p. 21 DEA/A. DAGLI ORTI/De Agostini Picture Library/Getty Images; p. 23 Duncan Walker/E+/Getty Images; p. 25 Gary Yeowell/The Image Bank/Getty Images; p. 27 Pavel K/Shutterstock.com; p. 29 Kevin Hellon/Shutterstock.com; p. 30 (Cerberus) Zvonimir Atletic/Shutterstock.com; p. 30 (Nemean lion) Pierre-Yves Beaudouin/Wikimedia Commons; p. 30 (Chimera) Leemage/Universal Images Group/Getty Images.

Printed in the United States of America

CPSIA compliance information: Batch #CS16GS: For further information contact Gareth Stevens, New York, New York at 1-800-542-2595.

MYTHICAL MONSTER

A woman with snakes for hair sounds like a character in a scary movie! That's the story of Medusa, but her tale is actually very old. It's a myth that's been told for more than 2,000 years!

BEYOND THE MYTH

A myth is a legend or story. The myth
of Medusa comes from Greece.

THE GORGONS

Medusa is one of the three Gorgons. The Gorgons were monsters and sisters of Greek myth who lived at the edge of the world near where the night came from. Medusa's sisters were named Sthenno and Euryale.

ALEREI ARCHITE TVR PLAS

BEYOND THE MYTH

"Gorgon" comes from an ancient Greek word
meaning "**fierce**" and "terrible."

MONSTROUS BEAUTY

One story of Medusa said she was born the only beautiful Gorgon. However, Athena, the goddess of war and wisdom, **punished** Medusa for not respecting her temple. Athena turned her hair into snakes!

BEYOND THE MYTH

Medusa was the only Gorgon who was
mortal, meaning she could be killed.

Another **version** of the Medusa myth says she was just as monstrous looking as her sisters! The Gorgons are said to have yellow wings on their backs, claws, and huge teeth. Medusa's sisters are said to have snakes on their bodies, too.

BEYOND THE MYTH

The name "Medusa" is an ancient Greek word that means "to guard."

PERSEUS

The myth of Medusa is part of the story about a famous Greek hero named Perseus. His father was Zeus, the king of the gods. Perseus and his mother lived on the island of Seriphos.

BEYOND THE MYTH

Before Perseus was born, his grandfather, Acrisius, was told a grandson would kill him. After Perseus was born, Acrisius sent him and his mother into the sea in a wooden box to try to stop this from coming true.

Seriphos's King Polydectes wanted to marry Perseus's mother, Danaë. Perseus didn't want him to! So, when Perseus was unable to bring a gift to a special dinner, Polydectes sent him away to get one—Medusa's head!

BEYOND THE MYTH

Polydectes didn't know Perseus was the son of a god. He didn't think Perseus would come back at all.

DANAË

15

GIFTS FROM THE GODS

Perseus needed some help. The messenger god Hermes gave him winged shoes. Hades, the god of the underworld, gave him a helmet that could make him **invisible**. Perseus also got a **shield** from Athena and a special sword.

BEYOND THE MYTH

Other versions of the myth say the Graiae helped
Perseus gather the tools he needed to kill Medusa.
They were the Gorgons' other sisters!

Using the special gifts from the gods, Perseus found the Gorgons' cave. Looking at them would turn him to stone, so he used Medusa's **reflection** in his shield to behead her. She was asleep and didn't fight back!

BEYOND THE MYTH

After Medusa was killed, her sisters tried to go after Perseus. He was wearing Hades's helmet, however, so they couldn't see him!

19

MEDUSA'S CHILDREN

Right after Perseus cut off Medusa's head, her sons Chrysaor and Pegasus were born from her neck! One writer said Chrysaor was born holding a golden sword. Their father was the god of the sea, Poseidon.

BEYOND THE MYTH

Pegasus was a winged horse featured in many other Greek myths. The hero Bellerophon caught Pegasus and rode him into battle.

21

TURNED TO STONE

Perseus placed Medusa's head into a special bag. Even dead, Medusa would still be able to turn people to stone! On his way home, Perseus used the head to turn a sea monster to stone and save a princess.

BEYOND THE MYTH

When Perseus returned to Seriphos, he used Medusa's head to turn King Polydectes into stone!

BLOOD TO SNAKES

As Perseus flew home on his winged shoes, Medusa's head was dripping blood from its bag. Myths say this blood fell on the country of Libya. Once it hit the ground, the blood created all the snakes there.

BEYOND THE MYTH

Another hero of Greek myth, Heracles, got a piece of Medusa's hair from Athena. He used it to guard the town of Tegea when enemies were attacking.

25

ATHENA

Most writers say Perseus gave Medusa's monstrous head to Athena. She put it on her shield to use in battle. Another myth says he buried the head in Argos, where he moved with his mother after his journey.

BEYOND THE MYTH

A famous statue in Florence, Italy, shows Perseus holding Medusa's head.

27

MONSTER ON GUARD

The myth of Medusa makes her sound like a monster! But pictures of her head became a symbol, or sign, to keep people safe. It was used on Greek and Roman shields and special necklaces called amulets.

VERSACE

BEYOND THE MYTH

The famous clothing line Versace uses
Medusa's head on their products!

29

Monsters of Greek Myth

CERBERUS
3-headed dog; guards the underworld

MEDUSA
hair of snakes; turns people to stone

NEMEAN LION
golden fur can't be cut; claws sharper than swords

SCYLLA
6-headed sea creature; attacks sailors who come near

CHIMERA
part lion, snake, and goat; breathes fire

FOR MORE INFORMATION

BOOKS

Hayes, Amy. *Medusa and Pegasus*. New York, NY: Cavendish Square, 2016.

Jantner, Janos. *Drawing Mythological Monsters*. New York, NY: PowerKids Press, 2013.

World Book. *Myths and Legends of Ancient Greece*. Chicago, IL: World Book, 2015.

WEBSITES

Monsters and Creatures of Greek Mythology

ducksters.com/history/ancient_greece/monsters_and_creatures_of_greek_mythology.php

Want more monstrous creatures? Check out this website!

Tales of Terror from Ancient Greece!

ngkids.co.uk/history/Greek-Myths

Learn more scary stories of ancient Greek myth!

Publisher's note to educators and parents: Our editors have carefully reviewed these websites to ensure that they are suitable for students. Many websites change frequently, however, and we cannot guarantee that a site's future contents will continue to meet our high standards of quality and educational value. Be advised that students should be closely supervised whenever they access the Internet.

fierce: showing strong feelings

invisible: unable to be seen

punish: to make suffer because of a wrongdoing

reflection: the creation of a picture as if by a mirror

shield: a piece of metal or wood used to guard the body in battle

version: a form of something that is different from others

INDEX